T0200850

HOLY HEATHEN

RHAPSODY

ALSO BY PATTIANN ROGERS

The Grand Array: Writings on Nature, Science, and Spirit

Wayfare

Firekeeper: Selected Poems, Revised and Expanded

Generations

Song of the World Becoming: New and Collected Poems, 1981–2001

The Dream of the Marsh Wren: Writing as Reciprocal Creation

A Covenant of Seasons

Eating Bread and Honey

Firekeeper: New and Selected Poems

Geocentric

Splitting and Binding

Legendary Performance

The Tattooed Lady in the Garden

The Expectations of Light

HOLY HEATHEN

RHAPSODY

———————————

PATTIANN ROGERS

PENGUIN POETS

PENGUIN BOOKS

Published by the Penguin Group
Penguin Group (USA) LLC
375 Hudson Street
New York, New York 10014

USA | Canada | UK | Ireland | Australia | New Zealand | India | South Africa | China
penguin.com
A Penguin Random House Company

First published in Penguin Books 2013

Copyright © Pattiann Rogers, 2013
Penguin supports copyright. Copyright fuels creativity, encourages diverse voices, promotes free
speech, and creates a vibrant culture. Thank you for buying an authorized edition of this book and
for complying with copyright laws by not reproducing, scanning, or distributing any part of it in
any form without permission. You are supporting writers and allowing Penguin to continue to
publish books for every reader.

Pages 95 and 96 constitute an extension of this copyright page.

LIBRARY OF CONGRESS CATALOGING-IN-PUBLICATION DATA
Rogers, Pattiann, 1940–
[Poems. Selections]
Holy Heathen Rhapsody / Pattiann Rogers.
pages cm. — (Penguin Poets)
Poems.
ISBN 978-0-14-312388-0
I. Title.
PS3568.O454H65 2013
811'.54—dc23   2013021082

Printed in the United States of America
1   3   5   7   9   10   8   6   4   2

Set in Fournier
Designed by Ginger Legato

For my husband, John, my sons, John and Artie,
my daughters-in-law, Lisa and Stacey, and my grandsons,
John, Abraham, and Moses, for the warmth and comfort
of their presence, home and hearth.

CONTENTS

I.

II.

III.

VIII.

IX.

X.

XI.

HOLY HEATHEN

RHAPSODY

Some of them are taproots, some
are spreading roots. With the quackgrass,
a sturdy rootstock. I recognize
the maneuvers: buried rhizomes
of beggar weed, long-sleeping seeds
of bitter dock. For canes and reeds,
they are leafy runners.

Their aim is true toward any sun-slit
opening in the multi-storied canopy,
any crack of clay or mortar, through
any ice-broken web across a boulder.
There's one now, a green squeeze through
the splinter seam in that fence post.

Up, outward, and into the deeps,
goosegrass, witch grass, panic
grass, crowfoot grass and nut grass.

And I've felt the keenness of their tactics,
haven't you? Spurs of bristlegrass,
milk thistle or sow thistle, needles, nettles
of sand bur, hooked spines, barbed
awns, bristly tufts. Blood can be proof.

Straining contrivances all—tangled
mats of knotweed and carpetweed,

swaying airy reach of wild vines (morning
glory, tack weed, grape), bold rankness
of burdock and tarweeds, plus the toadrush
love of slushy muck. Even mossy slime
has its loaded armies.

The slip and slither, the feint, twirl,
snatch, catch and hold. Which one
hasn't sought, pushed, striven,
probed, beseeched, bemoaned?

I know these ways, all of them,
angelic, obscene.

1.

Summer, everyday, the flurry-hover
of feeding hermit hummingbirds
and clearwing moths, bee-pause
and butterfly-flutter on shaking petals,
all those tongues lapping, licking,
and probing, the shiver and rub
of furry heads and bodies pushing
into the deepest crevices for nectar,
coming up dripping sugar and powdered
with pollen and off for the next one . . .

2.

Having grown up together, the lesser long-
nosed bat plunges perfectly with its bristly
tongue to sweep the sweetness of the saguaro
blossom. The hawk moth's tongue delves
its full length to reach exactly the far bottom
end of the comet orchid's narrow nectary.
Bumblebees with magic keys are everywhere
opening snapdragons with magic locks.

3.

In the early days of our beginnings,
when our first mothers came upon those colors
in the clearings—dawning pearl petals,
warm golds and startling scarlets, seductive

violets and dusky pinks growing in among
the monotonous greens—they were pleased.

Blossom perfumes rose spicy, winsome,
nostalgic with sun-and-moon fragrances.
The people fed, though the flowers were not
food, left them to bloom in the scratched-out
earth. Their seeds, mixed with the others,
were scattered and sown, season after season.

Though fragile, they thrived, all the while
cultivating deep in the bones of the people
the gentleness of care they required,
invoking in the genes of the people
a new longing for beauty.

The loveliest ones they wove
through the hair; the hardiest they placed
on the breasts; the favorites they enclosed
in the folded fingers of the dead.

4.
One of us could be the night pollinator,
flying with fur-covered wings of skin
north from Mexico over the rocky
slopes and seared bajadas of the deserts,
toward the mad musky fragrance

of the organ pipe cactus, its budding
flowers ripe and swelling in the dark.

The other one could be the blossom,
scented and sedate, the lightest shade
of lavender smooth as white waiting
in the night, ravaged, then graced,
pinioned on the tip of the tallest stem.

As if underwater, she floats and shimmies
slowly upward while the sun warms. She pauses
to sink again through the green and deeper
green garden leaves of this single tree,
its edifice all of Eden, earth and paradise,
slender branches bending and flowing
with the morning currents.

Summer lolls, lingers in its own mazes,
a white-limbed poplar, leafstalks, peel
of scented bark. Her body—seed wing
or feather down, thread slivers of silk—
touches each curled lobe and creviced branch
as she passes, slides underside, overside,
along the ridges and furrows. (Is that a tiny
tongue finding the way?) Love is this sun-
holding tree of lapping leaves, delves,
canopies, a multi-tangled cover.

A spasm of breeze, the tree shivers, each leaf
twisting white flash/green shadow. By will
or wind, she moves stemward toward the steady
trunk, following fissure and tangent, rests
finally folded in a woody niche. Who could
know better? Regard the celestial; the sky
is not shelter.

The sun is a total green of light
inside a single mimosa seed riding
inside the sky-green and river-
green of its buoyant pod canoe.
A black tern holds its feet flat
against its body as it wings

through the green skies and currents
of an earth winging through sizzling
star celestials. A ship, a speck
passing by above on the green
undersurface sky of the ocean, has no
notion of the volcanic flow seeping

from a sizzling crack in the earth
miles below, the only line of light
appearing on the ocean floor.
It could be a frond of fern sizzling
and spooling, unfurling its green
wing within the current and wake

of the day, the only frond of fire
appearing on the rain forest floor.
Remember the eye of the tern,
a speck of sky in which rides
for this moment the full wake
of summer and its green currents,

the spool of the sun in its dawning.
It could easily be a shawl of light
placed around a woman's shoulders
as she rests beneath a mimosa,
unaware of a seed drifting high
above her on the green undersurface

sky of July. See how the green fronds
of the rain unfurl, spooling away
in the ocean's current. Look again.
A crack appears across the universe
of a buoyant pod. The first throb
of the seed's green fire is dawning.

Once I saw a field of bluebonnets and fiery
paintbrush so solid with flowers it seemed
to be a surf and sea crests across which a ship
might sail petal by petal like a shadow passing
across an otherwise unbroken evening.

And I was the field, blue crests, stem
fire and surf. I was the shadow ship.
I was the evening passing. Everything
there in those moments was as inseparable
as the rhythm of the sea is inseparable
from the words of an old chanty sung
long ago by seamen inseparable
from a time no one now remembers.

At the shallow edge of a pond, I watched
an underwater nest of floating jelly-pod eggs,
a translucent, swayable heaven holding a thousand
eyes, bold dots of black, all seeing with one
flawless sight, and I was their vision.

I remember flying a summer migration,
each of us the flock indivisible, headed north
to breeding grounds. Paradise: our silver
feathered bodies, hearts and bones, solely
identical, all separate calls one single
sound emphatic. Our open wings were

the wheel and purpose of the sky turning
the earth exactly like the stars do.

That leaf indistinguishable—or that one
or that one, each magnificently anonymous—
is bound as an entire mountainside of autumn
aspen. Each yellow spinning is the piece
and the whole of the standing forest—alone,
unique, synonymous—moving with the Moving

that moves the aspen-altered wind and me.

A weaver, this spider, she plays her eight thin
black legs and their needle nail toes across
the threads faster, more precisely, than a harpist
at concert can pluck the strings in pizzicato.

Although blind at night, she nevertheless
fastens a thread to a branch of chokecherry
on one side of the path, links it to a limb
of shining sumac opposite, latches the scaffold
to ground stone and brace of rooted grasses.
And the structure takes dimension.

Skittering upside down across and around,
she hooks the hooks, knots the widening
spirals, the tightened radii, orbs and hubs,
bridges and bridgeheads. We can never hear
the music she makes as she plucks her silk
strings with all the toes and spurs and tarsal
tufts of her eight legs at once. She performs
the reading of her soul.

Oh, remember how vital her eyes, the eyes
of her gut, eyes of her touch gauging the tension,
her eyes of gravity and balance, of purpose,
steady eyes of reckoning. Don't miss
the moment when she drops, a quick grasp,
catches, swings forward again. An artiste.

She expands the sky, her completed grid
a gamble, a ploy played on the night. The silk
is still, translucent and aerial, hanging in a glint
of half-moon. The work is her heart strung
on its tethers, ravenous, abiding.

Listen . . . all white foxes, all white owls, all snowy
silver geese. Attend . . . all casual fish holding on
in the icy beads of a silver current. Snow leopards,
white bears, silver baboons, mottled white mice nosing
at autumn seeds . . . pause in unison, lift your heads.
Still your wings and heed . . . silvery blue moths fluttering
like flakes of moon. Long-haired, spike-horned goats
on precipitous cliffs, white spiderlings floating
mid-cloud . . . take note and remember. *Each barb*
of every feather, every black-tipped ivory hair, every
luminous scale and fan-like fin, each knuckle of spine
and nail, each red drop at the pith of the marrow,
at the root of all glare and mettle, every breath quiver,
every one, every single one, is beheld and declared.

I don't know if Jesus ever walked
in snow, through a storm of snow
blowing icy pieces stinging against
his face, in his eyes, snow melting
and freezing again in his hair until
it hung in stiff cords on his shoulders,
against his forehead. I've never seen
him pictured that way.

I don't know if he ever witnessed snow,
Jesus the Christ wrapped in robes that couldn't
keep out a winter wind of the mildest kind.
He would have had to swaddle his feet
and sandals in layers of cloth to walk through
the snow of a mountain pass, using his staff
along the narrows of slippery rocky paths.

Once in a May storm, I saw a hummingbird
hovering momentarily outside the window,
caught in a late spring freeze and snow-filled
fog. He was tiny iridescent feathers of green
and rose. He was a flittering bead of living color
taking off against the gray monument of winter.

I wonder if people would have followed
Jesus, climbing a mountain through the snow,
gathering around him there to listen, the wind
screaming its own beatitudes, whipping up

sudden gusts and shifts of snow descending
again over them like night. Hooded,
crouched down close together and sleeted
with snow, they might have resembled
a flock of sheep huddled on the hillside.

Once I saw a work of art lying abandoned
in the hoarfrost and snow of a forest clearing,
Van Gogh's *Starry Night* lying frayed among
the stiff and rattling grasses, that deep swirling
blue sky of bursting suns and splitting stars slowly
being buried by pearl on icy pearl of drift.

He could have told them the parable
of the blindness of snow-filled fogs
and white-outs, or the parable of the linking
prisms and patterns of any single flake,
or the parable of the transfiguration
by snow of needles, thorns, and jagged
stones. The breath of his words might
have been seen as a holy ghost of warmth
in the paralysis of that killing cold.

I don't know if Jesus ever witnessed snow.
It may never have snowed in Galilee,
although it is written that he rose
to heaven in "raiments white as snow."

Anything could appear to me here now,
walking in this obfuscation of snow and fog,
a true blizzard, if the wind were swifter.
Totally veiled, I move on legs I can't see,
parting endless screens and doorways
of chilling silk and ice-threaded smoke.

A black swan might float before me
at any moment, a hand's breadth
from my face, emerging suddenly
through this solid alabaster, a swan
so black it's a mere vacancy of bird,
a perfect absence of itself. I could easily
proceed, entering the fall of its body,
its wings spreading into their own deep
hollows as it vanishes with me.

And it seems altogether probable
that a white wagon hung with ivory
orchids and pale ferns and pulled by white
sea turtles could pass silently
above me, trailing slithers of pellucid
flying fish and ribbon eels twisting
through swells of icy dust.

Many crippled angels attend me here,
hovering on all sides. My breath,

the same color as this storm, floats
through their snow-filled wimples, swirling
their gauzy pantaloons. Coming in and out
of existence as I touch them, they regard me,
holding their muslin canopies over my head,
reciting prayers of blindness. In my vertigo,
I posit these angels now, not as beings,
but as fictions of time creating
the framework of a necessary place.

This dizzy loss, this dizzy loss is the same
loss, the same gain as dancing slowly
nowhere, eyes closed, with a boy I remember,
a boy who draws me closer, taking me in,
as a winter landscape filled with drowning
seas of descending snow takes in
and transfigures all previous boundaries.

Just now a christ with white eyes
touched my face. I felt the drift
of his hand across my forehead, his fingertips
brushing with Braille lightness once
along my cold lips blessing thus aloud
each and every one of his missing bones.

It has its places, in the grains of frigid gray
dust on the moon, in the descent of a barb
of feather lost from a jay, in a rasp of leaf
released by the sky and sinking to winter.
Distinctly present in a stone hand lying open

on rubble, in a clear glass marble embedded
in place of an eye, in the shorn hair of dead
women taken for wigs, it is itself and actual
across hillsides before threatening thunder
begins, in hollow, in cavity, in null,
on the surface of the lake where the heron's

wavering reflection lay before the heron rose
and disappeared. It is there in the workings
of wind around isolated spires of rock, through
abandoned trestles, picking at the rotted wooden
beams of condemned bridges, there among dry

tares and tarweeds, in any shard of buried
pottery, any crust of insect hull, any fragments
of crushed shell spilled like splinters of bone
thrown for dice on the sand, as the sun's dark
light in the east at dusk. In the steady haunting
waiting here and now, it is replicated and fact.

as an easy wind circumnavigating the land,
spreading slender grasses, their tawny sheaths
and dry bristles bending and swinging
in my wake, or lifting seeds, the keys of white
ash, the cottons of white poplar, carrying
their promises within my boneless presence;

to be a gusty wind in winter, an airy
cloud of resurrection raising the fallen
snow, surging skyward off an open hillside,
a swirling spiral of icy light circulating
within me like blood;

to bring the native fragrances of ripe
orchards, vineyards, and cedar oils,
the fecund damp of mountain rain forests
into the streets of the city, becoming myself
the odors of sweet perfumes, frying meat,
and liquors, the yeast of loaves rising
on their racks, smoke and steam my allies;

to give to the august and muted needles
of the piney woods sounds harmonious,
to release chords of voices inside the spires
of red rock corridors or make visible the art
of light in motion on dew-covered vines

of morning glories, or bestow leaping
pirouettes to languid dust of abandoned roads;

to be an easy wind smoothing the skin
of a lake at dusk, barely touching its radiance,
to pass over those waters as negligibly
as a shadow passes over the eyes, as silently
as the spirit of deliverance passes over each night
without notice, soothing, barely touching,
the hands and brows, the lips of the sleeping;

it could be grand—an eternal breath like the wind,
transcendent and old, to be in death always
ancient in the way the wind is always new.

When we meet now, we meet always
at dusk to play. The hard sun soothed,
easing off, is a mere sky of placid sea,
a pale plain of dimming blue and dun.

Even against the forest of walnut,
sassafras, and scrub oak hedging
our court, I can see his silhouette clearly,
as if he were a distinct piece of night
broken away, the sureness and potency
of night taken shape and set before me.
I imagine a greeting.

I serve. He receives. We play.
He's quick, anticipating me, meeting
each volley squarely. The *thonk* of the ball
found and sent speeding back and forth
is a smooth, fulfilling pleasure in the body,
as keen, as sweet as the swallow
of warm bread dipped in vinegar oil.

My aim determines his position; his return
predestines mine. I like what I become.
I adore his reckoning. More than once, I want
to jump the net and take him down. Pin
his shoulders. Kiss his face. Our game
is more than memory and prophecy.

Gradually the screen of trees dissolves,
disappears; or else the night expands,
absorbing the spaces inside each vein
and limb; or else the forest and the night
switch names, trade places. I lose sight
of him among the cast of stars.

His return comes from farther
and farther away, the thrust of the ball
sounding more and more of shadow,
its journey back to me a longer
and longer message. I can still judge

his angle, still hear the nuance
of his strategies. I know his study.

I dart forward, swing high,
send the next ball back with all
the might of my several minds, watch,
listen, ready in my stance, wait
for as long it takes.

Approaching two handspans from dusk,
he is an infinitesimal fraction of the day
concluding. As he looks west, his shadow
lays a line pointing due east. His spine
is as straight as the walking staff he carries.

He strolls through the center of a grassland,
seed-headed weeds and wild rye swirling
around him in a gold glinting wind. He walks,
as well, within the memory of a circle of fish
he once saw similarly swirling, a living ring
flashing silver in a silver sea.

He is three degrees northwest of madness,
three steps beyond glory, standing alongside
a bank of sunflowers up to their necks
in madness, up to their necks in glory.

He passes through a coordinance
of fragrances: yarrow, nectarine, salt,
a vagueness of myrrh. The presence
of his place is validated by a yellow-headed
blackbird who watches with its one
appropriate eye.

Reflecting an angle of attention, he pauses
as he attunes to the sounds of insects

chirring in the weeds of a rain-filled delve.
For a moment, he is located both inside
and outside his vision of finding that storied
baby hidden in a basket among water-filled
weeds and the sleepy strumming of crickets.
Would he take the infant up in his arms?

He gauges in the same way the spreading
branches of the fig tree calculate. His face
equals the sky he surveys. He enters the night.
He is more than the darkness as it dives away
backward now toward the soundless roar
of the stars appearing from all directions.

It could make a person dizzy,
those spinning, circling heavens filled
with knots of stars, swirling blue
stars approaching, blue-shadow stars
fading away. It's a mayhem of reeling,
a scattering blue dust of star clouds
circling the circling centers of spiraling
galaxies wheeling forever toward no
known horizon.

        Someone, immersed
in the deep beauty of these blue celestials,
could get lost while waiting for hands
to deliver perhaps an orange, perhaps
an apple, scarlet or gold, a sprig of green,
a blossom, pink dogwood, spring plum.

Inspired by "Golden Horn" Tondino
The Museum of Fine Arts, Houston, Texas

We feared this most in those days:
the black moon in a white sky.
On waning nights the glossy black
gleam of this moon's beauty inching
toward the west was a ponderous
pearl too heavy to admire.

During the nights of its fullness,
however, there was no lunacy
in the black moon but a lunar pall
pervading the countryside, touching
every hearth and field, as they say.
Any soul, inevitably so entered,
succumbed to that dearth. Remember
the wearisome wringing then.

And the hooded witch flowers
spawned by this moon in the damp
of midnight were no lilies. White
moths born of their black seeds
were the art of those blossoms,
foreboding their theme.

We feared the endless depth
of the black moon, the impenetrable
entryway to its wide-open tunnel,
the paralyzed swallow of its toothless

mouth. Is it true, an abyss can create
shadows of energy? We often found
dreams in the threat of the black
moon, in the same way as we often
heard voices coming from the empty
sockets of the graveyard skulls.

The black notes of the black moon's
music penned on parchment were
as vacant as the black dots of the stars
seen in their constellations against
the white night of the black moon

For the comfort of nostalgia, Maestro,
here is a coin. Play again the dirge
we danced to in those days.

The screeching cries
of the killdeer in the night create
their own narrow channels through the blades
of broken grasses and sharp-edged
dunes lining the shore.
Likewise,
the nightjar's whistle cuts a passage,
like a stream, across the open desert.
Only the nightjar knows the stars
of that passage, just as the limpkin's
wail is a direction only the limpkin forges
through the marshlands.
The furrows
of the field cricket's triplet chirps and shrill
courtship trills transform the sorrels
and doveweeds in the ditch, fashioning
needle ways and grids of space by the run
of their own notes.
And the thin cough-bark
of the bobcat establishes another sparse and arid
stalk among the rocks and brushy land where
it roots and withers.
No one can fully explore
the corridor made through the dark by the coyote's
jagged shrieks and clacking yaps, those yelping
howls like sheer descending cliffs, a noise
jumbled like rock-filled gulches and gulleys.

None but the coyote.

On icy plains, the snowy
owl occupies the cavern of its own silence,
a cavern formed by its quest for sweet blood
of lemming or hare. Within the polished,
black-and-white crystals of the freezing
night air, the owl watches from the warm
hollow of its stillness.

The inner eye of the Cat Goddess recites
without pausing the blood verses of foraging
mice written beneath a snow-covered field.

The Basking God of the lyre snake, red-
bellied snake, and blue garter snake
is explaining the coil of the galaxy.
The Upside-Down Creator of the nuthatch

descending the tree headfirst in circles
is willing the sky and toe hooks to hold tight,

and they do. Seers and Soothsayers are casting
lots at midnight to determine which beetle—
the elegant checkered, the nine-spotted
or two-spotted, the willow leaf, whirligig,
or harlequin cabbage—will be Lord Inheritor

of the Following Day. By her shifting, soaring,
rearranging, and scattering wisdom, the Prophet
of Autumn Winds makes visible the art
of the atom. And the Composer of the Sun's

Radiance is conducting the chords, the keys
and harmonies, of colliding ices and cold celestial
showers, flowing molten lavas and metals

and all migrating herds and tribes. She counts
the measures of the evening rains murmuring
like sleeping birds, numbers each single note
in the shimmering stanzas of Saturn's rings,
in finger cymbals, temple bells, and carillons,

and—there too—in the cadenza of the white
rose worn behind her ear.

except for the smallest white button
of mushroom leading the rank-and-file
up the rotting trunk of the oak, except for bulb,
corm, pip, and spore and the passive mien

of the autumn field when the off-kilter
scatter and skyward rattle of grasshoppers

have disappeared and except for the crowd
of acacia thorns pointing toward all destinations
possible in every direction out from the stem

center of their circumferences and aside
from the moss-and-mire covered bones
of stripped roots and crippled branches left
piled akimbo to molder among the beetles

in the sinless murk of the forest floor,
except for gorge, gulch, gully, and ravine,

except for the moment waiting in the fist
of the sycamore's tufted fruit and in the sting
of the loon's longing before it cries
and in the poise of the desert swallowtail
before it lifts from the dry mountain

wash and in the aim of the alligator's
undeviating glare before it swirls and sinks
in the generative and ancient slough, except

for the moment waiting in the green walls

of palm spikes, pendants and rosettes, knots
and currents of saw grasses and orchids,
in the tight weave and bloat of prayers

and weapons, in the moment before I move
out into the empty plain of the open sky silent
with sea-light, as if I were a wild and divine
thing myself, to be going I know not where.

Verses 6–10

6.

Deer passed the day quiet in this unmown
meadow. These grasses pressed to the earth
are the beds where they lay.

7.

My nose to the earth, I followed
the passing of the field mouse weaving
through the wheat grass, leaving seed husks
where she stopped to feed. I sniffed
the rank marking of the weasel's
passing on a rotting stump, rolled
in the scattered twigs and shell
remnants remaining after the passing-on
of the kingbird's nestlings, looked up
to the sky-scent and cry of the red-tailed
hawk sailing past overhead.

8.

Remember the only purely good man
to walk this earth? It could simply be
a wish contained in his myth that gardens
of tiny ferns, roseroot, and calamint,
meadow rue, white blossoms of baby's
breath, sprang up in the hollows
of his footprints, wherever he passed.

9.

A thin scarf of clouds draws itself slowly
over the face of the moon as the moon
passes over the stars and disappears behind
the arches of a stone gate, itself passing
with the earth through midnight and heading
toward the home that is morning.

10.

Like daylight passing through gold
glass beads stretched across a doorway
or the scent of wine grapes passing through
a latticed arbor or a feathering wind
passing through willows beside rippling
water passing through their shadows—
so a spirit, a ghost, a goblin, a god, created
and palpable, passes through every word
written, spoken, sung.

It might have been the million stars
on that night coming down silently
from their dark notches in the sky, bringing
with them only the light of fire, no flames,
no heat, no brimstone, and hovering there,
scattered through the swales and woodlands,
filling every space in the twining branches
and foliage of the forest around us.

Or maybe the sassafras, chinkapins,
and willows, the hollys, rushes, and wild
wheat, once every thousand years put forth
at midnight small buds of light lifting
and blinking like their own hearts in time
to the beat of the solstice. And we
were their witnesses.

Or perhaps it was a fleet of tiny invisible
ships, a multitude bearing flickering
lanterns on their masts, vessels launched
by beings searching the night's deep
current for their missing gods.

Or it might have been the black-winged
beetles of the order *coleoptera*, those fireflies
gliding slowly, almost floating, through
every space in the forest, above the dank

debris and murk of the earth, into the upper
canopies, igniting their wild bioluminescences,
each one throbbing with passion, drawing us
like spirits into the insect art of their being.

Yet, maybe those pulsing lights—drifting
low over the cow ponds and empty clearings,
pausing in among the forest corridors—
were the chantings of a peculiar prayer.
Had we been able to transcribe that shifting
syntax, decipher the counterpoint, join in with
the canticle, we might suddenly have become
ourselves—the lantern, the budding light,
solstice and wing, *time* and the *once upon*.

On the surface, it appeared
to be an osprey, a white-bellied raptor
with spiny talons, sentinel in its cottonwood
tower above rumbling water.

But diving suddenly, plunging hard,
it became a rapier splitting
the firmament with a deft slicing,
the sky slit through and falling open
from throat to navel.

Flapping then with wet frantic wings
through the breaking ripples and rapids
toward shore, its heavy silver catch held
tight in its claws, it was a messenger
clutching proof, dragging salvation
twisting and thrashing, out of the deep.

A fish, like time set down on a shore,
looks only two ways—one eye backward
toward life, the other forward toward sky.

I know an alchemist who is a churning
river transforming the heave and plummet
of light into the treadle of fins and gills.

In these moments this afternoon, god
is the sure glint of a flank below water,
and summons well; god is an osprey's empty
belly and receives with appetite; god
is fish spine and gut and relinquishes all.

This text seems right for a rushing
river full of gullets and bones, for its multiple
voices ring also with lies and devotions
that pitch and fall and swallow one another,
constantly present, suddenly lost,
all inseparable.

I know I said I loved you,
but I was drunk at the time
on citrus ice and marmalade.

I know I caressed the open places
where your petals join together
at the stem, but you just happened
to lean my way in the breeze,
into my hands already cupped
and blossom-shaped.

Maybe it seemed to you I reflected
the color of your grace in my eyes,
but it was evening, remember, the sun
sinking, and I was looking west.

And perhaps I did sing to you
of unfolding fringed petals
delicately crumpled first in the bud,
but it was really the unwinding
orange nub of the early evening
moon that I described with such rapture.
And if I did whisper to you once
of damp stamens, mesmerizing leaves
deeply lobed, spicy oil pockets
of seeds, those were merely facts,
a dull litany I recited in my sleep.

I don't know how you could think
I came of my own accord to lie
beside you all night in your sway.
I was only your imagination.

Don't ever believe I wrote these words
for you: *In those tangled, moist woods*
and thickets where I live, there grows
native and rooted deep in the desire
I myself invent, a divinely aloof,
double orange glory.

In love with the body, especially when
it dances in love with its own dance as it toes
and taps . . . flickers, creepers, chickadees
around a tree trunk, a click beetle in a flipping
somersault, the soft-shoe swish and sway
of the chee and feather grasses, the lissom uvas;

in love with the melding of the body,
especially when it languishes in the surf
of its own sleep . . . the belly slump of a leopard
stretched high on a branch, camouflaged,
leaf and fur, the tight sleep of a tumblebug egg
in its buried pod of dung, the man in a backyard
hammock slowly rocking with the slowly
rolling sun through evening shadows;

(so floats the sea otter on its back, bobbing
with the rocking sea, so bobs the gelatinous
umbrella and stinging strings of the jellyfish,
jelly and sting being the design and event
of the sea's own rolling body)

especially when the perfumes of a vigorous
body rocking, sleeping in the sun's evening
rest are of the salt of the sea, his body itself
being the salt of the earth, in love
with my mouth when the salt is tasted;

no ardor surpasses a body on the hunt,
halting abruptly, one foot lifted above the snow,
poised, as intent as frozen air, eyes as pure
and sharp as ice, then the bolt—the élancé—
beat and soul wholly in pursuit—the sail—
supreme the contact—most foreign, most
familiar, on the far edge of the horizon.

Some people, injured or frightened, rock
all day long holding their knees to their chins,
on sofas and wooden benches, in beds,
on bare floors, rocking as if they believed
they were trained riders on pearl stallions,
or golden-seeded stem-swingers in autumn
fields, or, with their eyes closed, believed
they were flowing purple flags in a sun-
warmed wind, convinced and comforted
by their own rocking.

Mary rocked a grown man dead in her arms,
and Lear swayed with Cordelia-gone held
close to his heart. Did they believe this old
motion performed long enough might
bring breath back? Or did they rock to ease
the loved, lapsing body into the earth?
Or did they rock to give their spines
and breasts a healing expression of grief?

Lullabies, cradles, rocking chairs, hammocks,
long rope swings—a need of the body seems
calmed by this motion of surge and release.

There's someone I want to take into my arms
tonight and rock, his head on my shoulder,
his lips at my throat. I want to move with him

easily, as moonlight rolls and rises on an open
sea, move with the same slow push and pause
a trout uses to tread snow water, the same delve
and release of a bird's tongue in a flume
of honeysuckle. Sinking and returning over
and over, I want to go with him backward
into the balm of stars, forward into the bible
of sun, swing through and behind the blind
bone mask together, out and beyond the cold
marble eyes, crossing and crossing back with him
in my arms until the name of any crossing,
the fear of any crossing, ceases to matter,
ceases to be, fall clear to the bottom of a death
with him, then rise together, saved by
that motion, and made whole, and restored.

It might be possible to disregard
the silent hiss of an open-mouthed
possum immobile on her silver back
in the forest leaves, and it might be
possible to view with indifference
the kite-like ears of a doe
hesitant at the edge of a sallow
muskeg, or the white, fleeing rumps
of over-the-prairie pronghorn.

Some people might never notice
the mating finch, the crimson
chimmer of his call, and some might
find it easy to dismiss the heaving
ribs of a spiny lizard at pause,
one forefoot raised, easy to pass by
indifferent to the ruffled blur
of a sage grouse rising
from the dusty brush.

And I can allow that not everyone
should be impressed with the unbalanced
and beadled claws of the ghost crab
or the multi-doored mound of a single
banner-tailed rat.

But the eyes met straight-on—
whether coyote yellow or sizzling bird-
bead of black metal, whether the tilted
study of gleaming lizard grain,
or the clear gray marble of seal,
or the dark unflickering candle
of fox—the eyes, nailhead-tenacious,
star-steady, searing as salt, unrelenting,
fierce pinions from far foreign realms,
surely no one can ignore being thus
so found and fixed, so disassembled,
so immediately redefined.

We are vulnerable to blindness caused
by the absence of light: snow-filled fog
along a frozen river at night, smoke stack
smoldering black clouds across the sun,
a burlap sack pulled over the head, fastened
with rope at the neck, eyes open inside
searching the weave for any pinpoint of day.

Death can happen by such blindness
when the lantern begins to flicker and dim
deep in a cave, fades, fails, and one is crawling now,
hands and knees on damp rock. All the cells
of the body—gut, fingertips, ends of the hair—
are straining to see. The nose sniffs for light.

King Harold II was blind to death, killed
by an arrow through his eye.

Once I saw a blind girl come to her door,
who couldn't see me as I stood on her lawn
watching the gray in the center of her brown
eyes, who, inside her blindness, saw in the stillness
how I held my breath to stay unseen, both
of us staring, susceptible to the absence of sight.

It can make the mind crazy to think of it:
how the generous light of the sun can penetrate

the eyes like a searing sword so harshly
brilliant that it creates total darkness, blinding,
cutting and killing, at the same time, sight
and the source of its own name.

Some, though having no eyes, are not blind.
The mimosa is not blind to the sun, leaning
upward toward its travel all day and also not blind
to the rain, swelling at its coming. Each blind
leaf partners with the eyeless wind.

Blindness is considered a virtue
in Justice, who has eyes we've never seen.

In a moment last spring, I was so vulnerable
to the call of a courting finch high on the roof
that I held in my hand unseen
not the bird but the sound of the bird.

The spiritual are susceptible to what is seen
in blindness. Closing their eyes, they can see
the cleaved stone in the spiral of the dayflower,
the green seed in the voice of night. Sometimes
they see (and therefore believe) the blind
god of the beginning whose closed eyes,
upon opening, created light.

Mangy bitch, emaciated,
old scavenger, pocked hide, warty
muzzle, one hip lower than the other,
she came to him by mistake (sent
by the Mistake Maker) straight
from the African plains
in a crate marked *The Unsightly.*

Cur-crone, she knows everything
about following lions, those regal
rumps, at a distance. She knows
about cowering, circling and circling,
the dart-in, the rip, and the snatch.
Snarling, ears back, half charging,
she's put to rout, in her time,
many worrisome vultures
and carrion crows.

By the neat nip of her teeth,
she's pulled fetid strings
of maggot-infested flesh
from abandoned hides;
once existed for a month
on the putrid marrow
from a wild boar's corpse.
She's lived in even leaner
times, leaping and munching

on lizards, grasshoppers,
and grubs.

Her eyes have seen the evening
sun setting on the Serengeti
from inside the boney cavern
of a fallen wildebeest.
She's called with others
beside a kill, yelped, howled
for murder's sake in chorus
all night long on the starless
grass sky of the savannah.

Forager, tenacious scrounger,
scarred, crippled
by the hooves of kicking
gazelles, she knows
better than anyone else
what kind of god it was
who left the pure white bone
of the moon picked so clean.

With scab worms and billy-club knots
on her rear, she's here—Thief, Felon,
Mongrel Messiah—beside the blind
beggar for good.

And now when his sustaining
visions of bonfires over water
come only dimly and rarely
when his fingertips harden, tough
and numb as leather and his beseeching
talents fail, when all sighted
angels face in the opposite
direction and there is no one
in that dark and frightening
paucity who sees
that he does not see,
then with his hand on her head,
she can lead him down these alleys
in the way he has to go.

no sound above a nod,
nothing louder than one wilted
thread of sunflower gold dropping
to a lower leaf

nothing more jarring
than the transparent slide of a raindrop
slicking down the furrow of a mossy
trunk

slightly less audible than the dip
and rock of a kite string lost and snagged
on a limb of oak

no message
more profound than December edging
stiffly through the ice-blue branches
of the solstice

nothing more riotous
than a cold lump of toad watching
like a stone for a wing of diaphanous
light to pass,

as still as a possum's feint

no message more profane than
three straws of frost-covered grass leaning
together on an empty dune

a quiet more
silent than a locked sacristy at midnight,
more vacant than the void of a secret
rune lost at sea

no sound, not even
a sigh the width of one scale of a white
moth's wing, not even a hush the length
of a candle's blink

nothing,
even less than an imagined finger held
to imagined lips

After a freight train lumbers by,
hissing steam and grumbling curses,
metal screeching against metal, it passes
into the night (which is the empty
shadow of the earth), becoming soft
clinking spurs, a breathy whistle, low
bells clanking like tangled chains,
disappearing as if on lambskin wheels.

Something lingers then in the silence,
a reality I can't name. It remains as near
to a ghost as the thought of a ghost
can be, hovering like a dry leaf spirit
motionless in a hardwood forest absent
of wind, inexplicably heraldic. It is closest
to the cry of a word I should know
by never having heard it.

What hesitates in that silence possesses
the same shape as the moment coming
just after the lamp is extinguished
but before the patterned moonlight
on the rug and the window-squares
of moonlight on the wall opposite
become evident. That shift of light
and apprehension is a form I should know
by having so readily recognized it.

After the yelping dog is chastened
and a door slams shut on the winter evening
filled with snow and its illuminations,
someone standing outside in the silence
following might sense not an echo
or a reflection but the single defining
feature of that disappearance
permeating the frigid air.

When all the strings and wires of the piano's
final chord are stilled and soundless, the hands
just beginning to lift from the keys, when the last
declaration of the last crow swinging down
into the broken stalks of the corn field ceases,
when the river, roaring, bucking, and battering
in its charge across the land, calms its frothy
madness back to bed at last, then suspended
in the space of silence afterward, may be
a promise, may be a ruse.

They float and sweep. They flicker
and unfold, having neither electrons
nor atoms, neither grasp nor escape.
Like skeletons, they could be
scaffolds. They are visible echoes.
Like scaffolds, they could be memory.
When of cattails and limber willows
on a summer pond, they are reverie.

Layering each other in a windy
forest, they can cover and disfigure
a face to a puzzle of shifting pieces.
If straight and unwavering when
crossing grassy lawns and clearings,
they are measures of time, true
of direction. The shadows
of minnows on the creek bed below
are either darting ripples of black
sun over the sand or reverse reflections
of surge as fish, design as soul.

They bring the devices and edicts
of winter, of spring, into the house,
over walls, ceilings, staircases—
the inside motion of a blossom falling
outside, a bird beyond the window
swooping a passage of pure flight

through the room. Shadow-drops
pearl over sofa, table, books, replicating
rain lingering in gold among leaves
and branches at dusk.

I sit on the floor within the shadow
network of a winter elm, its architecture
spread across the rug. The substance
of this structure is less than the bones
of a bumblebee bat, yet it holds me.

Some shadows are much esteemed,
those of canopies, awnings, and parasols.
Many ancient tales record sightings
of ostriches seeking the black relief
of cloud shadows on the savannah,
following them across the treeless plains
like magi following the holy star.

Maybe the metals of meteors, the drifting
remnants of galactic debris, the ices
and gravels of disintegrating comets
in their orbits cast showers of tiny pale
shadows (like spells or blessings or praises
upon us) as they pass between sun and earth.

With no fragrance—neither spicy, sweet,
acrid, nor mellow—without sighs or summaries,
without an aim of their own, like wraiths
and ghosts with no heft of any kind—the sole
matter of shadows is lack. Disappearing
in darkness, they depend for their being
on light. Therefore, they cannot be evil.
Some people still do not believe.

Sound with the cries of Rachel's children.
Moan over empty hillsides and river runnels,
among the broken stones of abandoned streets
and fallen fences, through empty channels
and sharp-ledged ravines resonant with echo.

Rasp and rattle with the integrity of a perfect
reckoning down the metal roof onto the splash
pans of gutters, down the pipes of open sewers.

Snore skywide with sporadic mumbles.
Rumble from your own soul sources.

Stutter erudite nonsense, a stentorian
preaching from high altars, pellets clicking
and tapping among the leathery leaves
of oak and hickory in the upper towers
of the kingly forest.

Is that the giggling of lost Peter and Aaron
pattering on the cold lake's surface?

Speak, an eloquence devoid of message
in the silence of floating fog. I'm listening,
the voice sinking among the invisible
blades of the morning marsh.

Tarry awhile in the dark, humming the sleep
and lullaby common to that far place
from which you have come.

In retreat, challenge slowly in single words
striking randomly: *now, and now, now,
now and now.*

In the dust, spit large rounded vowels.

Our Father, who is the Passageway in the tunnel
of the worm and the trench of the mole,
in the wintering eggs of the luminous beetle
and the ragged reachings of all roots scraggly

and crooked with the network of their knitted
inroads, who is the Deep in unseen subterranean
rivers, the Porous of limestone, sandstone,
and gravel through which groundwater seeps

to purity downward, the Sunless in buried aquifers,
and the overpowering Weakness in the single cell
enormities surmounting there, who is the Source
and Savior of the eyeless eel and the eyeless

pseudoscorpion and is the Blindness of the eyeless
eel and the eyeless pseudoscorpion, and the rigid
Seriousness of ancient cave chambers, echoing
caverns, and catacombs, damp stone spires

and walls of granite organs, the Light of calcite
pinnacles which, after touched by sudden light
in their lasting darkness, emit light themselves,
dimly, briefly, who is the seething core Intensity

of molten metals, the center Clench of solid
iron/nickel fury, who is the complete Circumference,

each and every inner Radius of orbital earth,
hallowed and empirical, who is the Story
and is the Telling and is the Silence beyond
forever. Amen.

Rain comes in its minions, streaming
down into ravines and rimples, running
over and under bedrock and boulders,
down the slopes of gulleys, sopping
mossy dells and frond-filled valleys.

And snow, without blizzard, colorless
with silence, floats to earth, gathering
across plains and lowland forests, covering
the smallest flat pads of weathered
mushrooms, filling the upturned hulls
of spent pods—yucca, locust, pea, mimosa.

All of these seek the earth.

Spiders drop too, sometimes sailing
in hatchling clusters, gliding through
a still day on streamers or blown
sideways over fallow fields until
the wind ceases and they settle
in the bristled grasses and mayweeds.

Whispy seeds of ash and maple aim
for it, each balanced with the wind on double
paper wings. Every direction points
finally toward earth. Acorns, walnuts,
hickories split away, plummet hard,

knocking through tangled twigs
and branches to get here.

And geese zero in, whiffling and skidding
feet first to a lake-slide landing, skimming
in praising sprays of water. Watch.

The earth is so desired. Coming
as close to it as possible, consumed by it,
white toads and blind fish adore the deep
of its internal damp, foregoing color for it,
relinquishing sight. The inert seek it too,
bone splinters, fleshy crumbs, nasty orts
and roughages sink through sea currents
all the way down to its bottom sunless bed.

The heavenly—angels, arch-angels—
deliberately descend, perching and hovering.
Their choruses sound then like broken chords
of wind strumming through pinyon pines,
like the dodecahedron ring of icy chimes
hanging in crystals from winter eaves.

With all the vast freedom and void
of the universe to select from, frigid evil
comes too, seeking warmth in the belly

of the lover, power in the birthright of the sea,
spring light in the pulse of the prairie.

The earth is so desired. How its rock
and river body is loved, its dune and hillock,
its night and day demeanor. Even the dead—gone,
buried, and forgotten—take its name forever.

ACKNOWLEDGMENTS

With thanks for the tenacious and devoted work of the editors of the following journals in which the poems listed were first published, and thanks to the editors of all such journals and magazines that provide venues for the publication of poetry.

American Scientist: "Holy Heathen Rhapsody"

ARTline: "Blue Heavens"

Ecotone: "Co-evolution: Seduction"; "Summer's Company (Multiple Universes)"

Field: "Scarlatti Sonata Testament"

Georgia Review: "At Work"; "Night and the Creation of Geography"; "Yearning Ways"

Image: "Hail, Spirit"; "Speak, Rain"

The Iowa Review: "Edging Dusk, *Ars Poetica*"; "In the Silence Following"; "Less Than a Whisper Poem"

Literature and Belief: "The Snow of Things"; "What Existence"

New Mexico Poetry Review: "The Earth Without a Spiritual Dimension"

Orion: "Romance"

Poetry International: "The Doxology of Shadows"

World Literature Today: "Signifying (Coming to Earth)"; "The Body Entire"

My thanks to the editors of the following chapbooks in which certain poems in this book appeared: *Lies and Devotions* (Tangram Press) and *Summer's Company* (Brooding Heron Press).

I'm extremely grateful to Paul Slovak for his kindness, his efficient editing, and his insightful and helpful comments on my manuscript.

PHOTO BY JOHN R. ROGERS

Pattiann Rogers has published eleven books of poetry and two collections of essays. Her most recent books are *The Grand Array: Writings on Nature, Science, and Spirit* (Trinity University Press, 2010) and *Wayfare* (Penguin, 2008). *Song of the World Becoming: New and Collected Poems 1981–2001* (Milkweed Editions) was a finalist for the Los Angeles Times Book Prize and an Editor's Choice in *Booklist*. *Firekeeper: New and Selected Poems* was a finalist for the Lenore Marshall Award and a *Publishers Weekly* Best Book of 1994. Rogers is the recipient of two NEA Grants, a Guggenheim Fellowship, and a 2005 Literary Award in Poetry from the Lannan Foundation. Her poems have won three prizes from *Poetry*, the Theodore Roethke Prize from *Poetry Northwest*, two Strousse Awards from *Prairie Schooner*, and five Pushcart Prizes. Her work has appeared in *Best American Poetry* in 1996 and 2009, and in *Best Spiritual Writing*, 1999, 2000, 2001, 2002, and 2010. Rogers's papers are archived in the Sowell Family Collection of Literature, Community, and the Natural World at Texas Tech University. She has been a visiting writer at numerous universities and colleges and was an associate professor at the University of Arkansas from 1993–97. She is the mother of two sons and has three grandsons. She lives with her husband, a retired geophysicist, in Colorado.

PENGUIN POETS

JOHN ASHBERY
Selected Poems
Self-Portrait in a Convex
  Mirror

TED BERRIGAN
The Sonnets

LAUREN BERRY
The Lifting Dress

JOE BONOMO
Installations

PHILIP BOOTH
Selves

JULIANNE BUCHSBAUM
The Apothecary's Heir

JIM CARROLL
Fear of Dreaming:
  The Selected Poems
Living at the Movies
Void of Course

**ALISON HAWTHORNE
DEMING**
Genius Loci
Rope

CARL DENNIS
Callings
New and Selected Poems
  1974–2004
Practical Gods
Ranking the Wishes
Unknown Friends

DIANE DI PRIMA
Loba

STUART DISCHELL
Backwards Days
Dig Safe

STEPHEN DOBYNS
Velocities: New and Selected
  Poems, 1966–1992

EDWARD DORN
Way More West: New and
  Selected Poems

ROGER FANNING
The Middle Ages

ADAM FOULDS
The Broken Word

CARRIE FOUNTAIN
Burn Lake

AMY GERSTLER
Crown of Weeds: Poems
Dearest Creature
Ghost Girl
Medicine
Nerve Storm

EUGENE GLORIA
Drivers at the Short-Time
  Motel
Hoodlum Birds
My Favorite Warlord

DEBORA GREGER
By Herself
Desert Fathers, Uranium
  Daughters
God
Men, Women, and Ghosts
Western Art

TERRANCE HAYES
Hip Logic
Lighthead
Wind in a Box

NATHAN HOKS
The Narrow Circle

ROBERT HUNTER
Sentinel and Other Poems

MARY KARR
Viper Rum

WILLIAM KECKLER
Sanskrit of the Body

JACK KEROUAC
Book of Sketches
Book of Blues
Book of Haikus

JOANNA KLINK
Circadian
Raptus

JOANNE KYGER
As Ever: Selected Poems

ANN LAUTERBACH
Hum
If in Time: Selected Poems,
  1975–2000
On a Stair
Or to Begin Again
Under the Sign

CORINNE LEE
PYX

PHILLIS LEVIN
May Day
Mercury

WILLIAM LOGAN
Macbeth in Venice
Madame X
Strange Flesh
The Whispering Gallery

ADRIAN MATEJKA
The Big Smoke
Mixology

MICHAEL MCCLURE
Huge Dreams:
  San Francisco and
  Beat Poems

DAVID MELTZER
David's Copy:
  The Selected Poems of
  David Meltzer

ROBERT MORGAN
Terroir

CAROL MUSKE-DUKES
An Octave Above Thunder
Red Trousseau
Twin Cities

ALICE NOTLEY
Culture of One
The Descent of Alette
Disobedience
In the Pines
Mysteries of Small Houses

LAWRENCE RAAB
The History of Forgetting
Visible Signs: New and
  Selected Poems

BARBARA RAS
The Last Skin
One Hidden Stuff

MICHAEL ROBBINS
Alien vs. Predator

PATTIANN ROGERS
Generations
Holy Heathen Rhapsody
Wayfare

WILLIAM STOBB
Absentia
Nervous Systems

TRYFON TOLIDES
An Almost Pure Empty
  Walking

ANNE WALDMAN
Gossamurmur
Kill or Cure
Manatee/Humanity
Structure of the World
  Compared to a Bubble

JAMES WELCH
Riding the Earthboy 40

PHILIP WHALEN
Overtime: Selected Poems

ROBERT WRIGLEY
Anatomy of Melancholy and
  Other Poems
Beautiful Country
Earthly Meditations: New
  and Selected Poems
Lives of the Animals
Reign of Snakes

MARK YAKICH
The Importance of Peeling
  Potatoes in Ukraine
Unrelated Individuals
  Forming a Group Waiting
  to Cross

JOHN YAU
Borrowed Love Poems
Paradiso Diaspora